# Njalo

A Collection of 16 Hymns in the African Tradition

by Patrick Matsikenyiri

Edited by Dan Damon

Foreword by C. Michael Hawn

Abingdon Press
Nashville

# Foreword

A major shift in Christianity has taken place since the mid-twentieth century. In 1950, two-thirds of the Christian community lived in North America and Europe. Today, two-thirds of the worldwide Christian community lives in the Southern hemisphere. Every 24 hours there are 3,000 fewer Christians in the Euro-North American context and 16,000 new Christians in the Southern hemisphere!

The work of the missionaries in the nineteenth and twentieth centuries has born much fruit. Missionaries from Europe and North America took their own songs to the mission field and people around the world sing "Amazing Grace" and "A Mighty Fortress Is Our God." Now we are privileged to experience sung prayers from the Southern church—songs reflecting Christianity that have germinated in the soils of Africa, Asia, Latin America, and Oceana.

Patrick Matsikenyiri is the product of music missionaries to Zimbabwe, such as Olof Axelsson and Henry Weman from the Church of Sweden (Lutheran), and Mennonite Robert Kauffman and Methodist John Keammer from the United States. These missionary voices from the Northern world nurtured Patrick in the 1960s, 1970s, and 1980s, helping him discover his Zimbabwean voice. Patrick has carried his songs throughout the world as an *animateur* (song animator) for the World Council of Churches, as a teacher in a wide variety of international venues, and through his students at Africa University.

Producing a book like this is a cross-cultural endeavor. I cannot think of a better North American partner than Dan Damon. Dan has provided very singable English translations that are both natural and reflect the meaning of the original Shona. Together, Patrick and Dan have provided a volume with a variety of worship expressions, including songs of praise ("Baningyeti Bayawe"), thanksgiving ("Wonai"), invocation ("Mweya Mutsvene Uyai Pano"), and commitment ("Ndai Wona Hama Yakanaka"). These songs also bear the brokenness of Zimbabwean society where so many people live under the burdens of political oppression, economic turmoil, family brokenness, and the scourge of HIV/AIDS. See especially "Zviro Zvacho Zvanyanya."

So, sing and dance in faith and solidarity with Christians from Zimbabwe. As the Shona proverb says: "If you can talk, you can sing. If you can walk, you can dance."

C. Michael Hawn
Professor of Church Music
Perkins School of Theology
Southern Methodist University
Dallas, Texas

# Contents

# Njalo
## *(Always)*

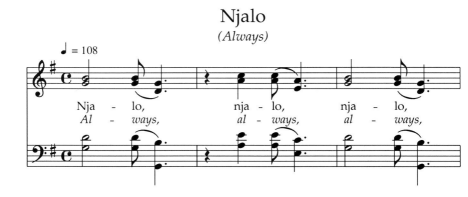

Nja - lo, nja - lo, nja - lo,
*Al - ways, al - ways, al - ways,*

nja - lo, nja - lo, nja - lo,
*al - ways, al - ways, al - ways,*

*Fine*

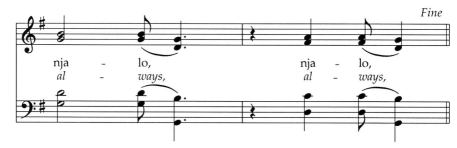

nja - lo, nja - lo,
*al - ways, al - ways,*

WORDS: Ndebele, Zimbabwe; English trans. by Patrick Matsikenziri
and Daniel Charles Damon
MUSIC: Ndebele, Zimbabwe; arr. by Patrick Matsikenyiri

NJALO
88.86.86

Always, we pray and do all kinds of chores and activities as the Lord leads us. Jesus is the leader who never fails. The Lord will always try to do his best for his sheep.

5

# Baba Tino Tenda
## *(God, We Thank You)*

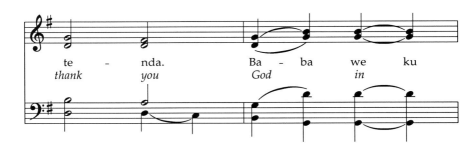

WORDS: Trad. Shona, Zimbabwe; English trans. by Patrick Matsikenyiri
and Daniel Charles Damon

MUSIC: Trad. Shona, Zimbabwe; arr. by Patrick Matsikenyiri

Trans. and arr. © 2006 Abingdon Press, admin. by The Copyright Co.

BABA TINO TENDA
Irr.

This is a prayer commonly used as a blessing for a meal. You can say it and you can also sing it in Shona and in English. The song reflects our gratitude to God for his care during our days on earth and that we are also grateful for the food that has been accorded to us at this point in time.

# Mambo Jesu Achiwoneka
### (If the Lord Would Appear Before Me)

Mam-bo Je-su a-chi-wo-ne-ka
*If the Lord would ap-pear be-fore me,*

a-chi-wo-ne-ka
*ap-pear be-fore me,*

nda-i-zo ga-ra na-ye, nda-i-zo
*I know I'd stay right with him, I know I'd*

ga-ra na-ye,
*stay right with him,*

ga-ra na-ye, nda-i-zo ga-ra na-ye.
*stay right with him, I know I'd stay right with him.*

ga-ra na-ye, ga-ra na-ye.
*stay right with him, stay right with him.*

WORDS: Trad. Shona, Zimbabwe; English trans. by Patrick Matsikenyiri
and Daniel Charles Damon
MUSIC: Trad. Shona, Zimbabwe; arr. by Patrick Matsikenyiri
Trans. and arr. © 2006 Abingdon Press, admin. by The Copyright Co.

ACHIWONEKA
Irr.

If Jesus were to be physically seen I would stay with him. This song reminds us of the faith that Lazarus' sisters, Martha and Mary, had in Jesus when they said that if Jesus would have been present, their brother would not have died (John 11:32). As the song progresses, faith becomes the center pole of belief in God.

# Ariko Narini
## (He Is There Forever)

WORDS: Trad. Shona, Zimbabwe; English trans. by Patrick Matsikenyiri
and Daniel Charles Damon

MUSIC: Trad. Shona, Zimbabwe; arr. by Patrick Matsikenyiri

ARIKO NARANI
66.66D

8

Some time ago one of the commissions in the World Council of Churches (WCC) asked me to lead music at one of their seminars in Kenya. The seminar was putting together material for the 8th Assembly of the WCC, which was coming up in the year 1998. We had a drama of life after death prepared for one of the sessions. During our preparation, the imagery of the Lord now and forever in heaven captured my imagination and completely filled my mind. In the process I was inspired to write the song "Ariko Narini" (*He Is There Forever*): call on Jesus, he is there forever, call on him, he is there forever.

# Baningyeti Bayawe

*(Let Us Praise the Lord Our God)*

Ba-ning-ye - ti Ba - ya-we. Ba-ning-ye - ti Ba - ya - we.
*Let us praise the Lord our God. Let us praise the Lord our God.*

Ban - ning - ye - ti Ba - ya - we. A - men.
*Let us praise the Lord our God. A - men.*

Ba-ning-ye - ti Ba - ya - we. Ba-ning-ye - ti Ba - ya-we.
*Let us praise the Lord our God. Let us praise the Lord our God.*

WORDS: Trad. Cameroon; English trans. by Patrick Matsikenyiri
MUSIC: Trad. Cameroon; arr. by Patrick Matsikenyiri

BANINGYETI
77.72D with
Hallelujahs

Trans. and arr. © 2006 Abingdon Press, admin. by The Copyright Co.

This traditional song, based on a Cameroon text, focuses on the praise of God who cares for us in our daily lives. The "Haleluya" highlights the climax of our gratitude. Expression of joy is evident when people join together in the chorus with hands waving in the air accompanied by dance to the song.

# Hakuna Wakaita sa Jesu
## (There's No One in This World Like Jesus)

Ha - ku - na wa - kai - ta sa Je - su, ha -
*There's no one in this world like Je - sus, there's*

ku - na wa - kai - ta sa - ye; ha - ku - na wa - kai - ta sa
*no one in this world like him; there's no - one in this world like*

Je - su, ha - ku, ha - ku - chi - na.
*Je - sus, there's no one, there's no one like him.*

WORDS: Trad. Shona, Zimbabwe; English trans. by Patrick Matsikenyiri
and Daniel Charles Damon

MUSIC: Trad. Shona, Zimbabwe; arr. by Patrick Matsikenyiri

HAKUNA WAKAITA
Irr.

Trans. and arr. © 2006 Abingdon Press, admin. by The Copyright Co.

Nda - mha - nya, mha - nya, kwe - se, kwe - se. Nda -
*I'm run - ning, run - ning, search - ing, search - ing. I'm*

te - nde re - ra, kwe - se, kwe - se. Nda -
*turn - ing, turn - ing, search - ing, search - ing. I'm*

tsva - ka, tsva - ka, kwe - se, kwe - se, ha -
*search - ing, search - ing ev - ery - where. There's*

ku, ha - ku - chi - na.
*no - one, there's no - one like him.*

This song tries to show that Jesus is above human beings in his care for people of the earth. No one on this earth can be equal to Jesus, he is the supreme person in all our daily lives. We have tried to run everywhere without finding someone like him. We tried to turn around hoping to find someone; that failed as well. We have kept on searching everywhere to no avail. The song has created a sense of ecumenism in many churches, which are using it with movements that depict the meaning of the text. The song becomes more effective when you actually reflect the meaning of the words through the motions.

# Kuti Ndisine Rudo
## (If I'm Without Love)

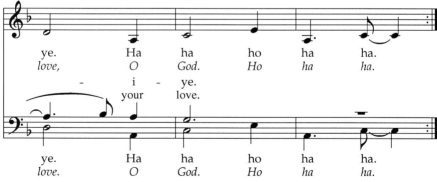

*This piece begins with the congregational ostinato, which continues as the descant and stanzas alternate. The song ends with the congregational ostinato. The hosho (shaker) plays quarter notes throughout. The joyful sounds ho, ha and woyé need no translation.*

WORDS: Patrick Matsikenyiri; English trans. by Patrick Matsikenyiri
and Daniel Charles Damon (1 Cor. 13)
MUSIC: Patrick Matsikenyiri

RUDO
Irr.

Trans. and arr. © 2006 Abingdon Press, admin. by The Copyright Co.

14

*Soprano descant (sung over congrgational ostinato, alternatively with stanzas)*

Ka  na  ndi - chi - tau - ra  nge - mi  tau -
*If    I    speak  in    the tongues,   mor - tal    and*

ro  ye - va - nhu  ne - ngi - ro - si  ha
*an - gel,    if   I    speak   in    these   tongues   with -*

ndi - si - ne  ru -  - do,  ndi - ri
*out    love,   with - out    your  love,    I    am*

ku - fa - na - na  ne - sa - fu - ri  ne - da -
*on - ly    a   gong,   nois - y    and    use - less,   a*

re  ri - no  ri - ra  nha -  ndo.
*cym - bal   that's   clang - ing    a -    way.*

15

*Leader (sung over congregational ostinato)*

1. Ku-nya - po - ro - fi - ta (a) ne - ku - zi - va kwe - se
*If I know ev - ery-thing, proph - et and schol-ar com-bined,*

ha wo - ye wo - ye, ku - ti ndi - si - ne ru -
*ha wo - ye wo - ye, I am noth-ing with-out*

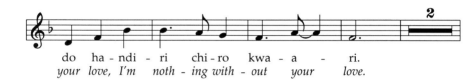

do ha - ndi - ri chi - ro kwa - a - ri.
*your love, I'm noth - ing with - out your love.*

Ku-nya - i - te mu-tsa zva - ngu ku - gu-tse va - ro -
*If I give all I have, feed - ing the poor at my door,*

mbo wo - ye wo - ye, ku - nya -
*love is still need - ed. If I*

pi - re mu - vi - ri ha - zvi - ndi ba - tsi - ri wo.
*give up my own bod - y with - out love, I fall short.*

16

2. Chi-zwa zvi-no ma-ba - sa ar - wo ru-do rwa Ba -
*As we lis-ten, we learn what love is do-ing for God's*

ba Mwa - ri _____ ru-no ti - wa ne-mu -
*child - ren here: ___ love is pa-tient, it is*

tsa ha - ru - ne sha-nje (a) Ha - ru - da - di.
*kind and God's love is not proud, nev - er jeal - ous;*

Ha-ru - tsva-ki zvi-ro zva-rwo ha - ru-za - ri-dzwe -
*it does not seek its own way, and re - sent-ful it will*

wo nha - ndo, ___ ru-no fu - ki - dza zve -
*nev - er be; ____ it bears all things, it be -*

se ru - no - da - wi - ra zvi - ro zvo zve - se.
*lives all things, love hopes and en - dures all that comes.*

17

*Leader (sung over congregational ostinato)*

3. Ru-no - si-mbi - ra zve - se ne - ku - ti-wa mu-zvi-
*Love is  pa-tient in  all  things, in  life's   tri-als  we know*

ro  sve - se. ___
*love won't  fail. ___*

Ru-no - dzi-dzi - sa  u -
*Love is   show-ing  the world*

pe - nyu  hu - tsve-ne  pa-mhe - ne - wo. ___
*how   to   live   dai - ly   in God's  free - dom. ___*

Ru - no - tsa - dza - nu - ra   nzi - ra  ye - kwe-nde ku-de -
*We know  God's love   is  now  break - ing  each   hur - dle   on our*

nga dzve - ne. ___
*jour - ney   home. _*

Ru - no - si-mbi - sa  u -
*We know   love is    a great*

sha-mwa - ri   hwe du - na Je - su  Te - nzi  we - du. _
*pow - er   that  binds us  in  a  friend-ship with  Je - sus. _*

RUDO (1 Corinthians 13) is one of my early serious compositions. I listened to a sermon on a Sunday. The preacher (a pastor from a different circuit) was so powerful in his delivery that the sermon stuck with me the whole day. That Sunday evening at midnight I woke up and wrote the congregational response in tonic solfège. I went back to bed. About an hour later I woke up and did the lead descant and went to bed. Early Monday morning as headmaster I gathered my staff members in one of the classrooms and gave them parts to sing and recorded that segment.

During the day I would play back the recorded music and began to construct the verses based on the text in the Bible. The following day Dr. Kaemmer visited me from Nyadiri Mission. We then got the staff together and sang the whole song with me doing the leader's part. Dr. Kaemmer then recorded the whole song and took it away to Nyadiri where he started putting it into staff notation. I love this piece, RUDO, because it became my turning point to added interest in composition.

# Pano Handiwo Musha

## (This Is Not Our Homeland)

WORDS: Patrick Matsikenyiri; English trans. by Patrick Matsikenyiri
and Daniel Charles Damon

MUSIC: Patrick Matsikenyiri; transcribed by Eileen Guenther

PANO
77.57 with Refrain

Ho, Ho Ba - ba we,
*O God ___ of all.*

mu - sha, si - mu - ka toe -
*home - land, let us rise and*

ha - ma, si - mu - ka toe -
*pil - grims, let us rise and*

**1** Pa - no,
*This land,*

**2** Zvi - no - ndo - fa - mba,
*Now I'm walk - ing,*

**1** nda.
*go.*
nda.
*go.*

**2** nda.
*go.*

*Refrain*

Ndo - fa - mba, ndo - fa - mba, ndo - fa - mba, ndo - fa - mba,
*Now I am walk - ing, now I am walk - ing,*

This song reminds us this world is just a temporary shelter for our life. A home has been made ready for us in heaven. When you sing "ndofamba ndofamba," a steady, confident walk should be employed to create a sense of assurance that we are walking toward our goal: our everlasting home in heaven.

# Mweya Mutsvene Uyai Pano

*(Holy Spirit, Come By Here)*

Mwe - ya M'tsve - ne, Mwe - ya M'tsve - ne,
*Ho - ly Spir - it, Ho - ly Spir - it,*

Mwe - ya M'tsve-ne u - yai pa - no. Mwe - ya M'tsve-ne,
*Ho - ly Spir - it, come by here. Ho - ly Spir - it,*

Mwe - ya M'tsve-ne, Mwe - ya M'tsve-ne u - yao pa - no.
*Ho - ly Spir - it, Ho - ly Spir - it, come by here.*

WORDS: Trad. Shona, Zimbabwe; English trans. by Patrick Matsikenyiri
and Daniel Charles Damon

MUSIC: Trad. Shona, Zimbabwe; arr. by Patrick Matsikenyiri

MWEYA MUTSVENE
LMD

Trans. and arr. © 2006 Abingdon Press, admin. by The Copyright Co.

Mwe - ya M'tsve-ne,     Mwe-ya M'tsve-ne,     Mwe-ya M'tsve-ne,
*Ho - ly Spir - it,*     *Ho - ly Spir - it,*     *Ho - ly Spir - it,*

Mwe - ya M'tsve - ne,     Mwe - ya M'tsve - ne,
*Ho - ly Spir - it,*     *Ho - ly Spir - it,*

Mwe - ya M'tsve-ne,     Mwe - ya M'tsve-ne u - yai pa - no.
*Ho - ly Spir - it,*     *Ho - ly Spir - it,   come by here.*

This song invokes the Holy Spirit to come and be with us as we worship and do our daily chores. When sung with conviction, it creates an atmosphere that compels the congregation to have one mind. The song reminds us of the disciples during the Transfiguration when they ended up with one mind, telling Jesus that they should stay put since the heavenly friends had joined them and the situation was great.

# Namatai
## (Shepherd God, to You We Pray)

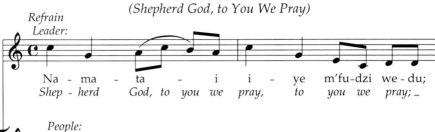

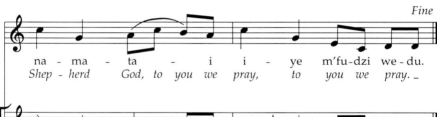

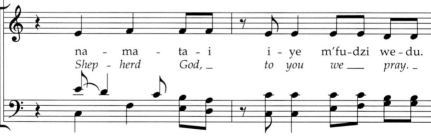

WORDS: Patrick Matsikenyiri; English trans. by Patrick Matsikenyiri
and Daniel Charles Damon

MUSIC: Patrick Matsikanyiri; arr. by Patrick Matsikenyiri

NAMATAI
Irr.

I wrote this song at a workshop in a village high school outside of Bulawayo, Zimbabwe. While it was fresh from the pot, the students were singing it on the bus. They loved it and sang it all the way home to Kwanongoma College of Music in Bulawayo. This song invites people to be in persistent prayer. The song shows that God always knew that divisions in life would be evident, so he sent his only begotten Son to redeem the world. Therefore we need to pray and worship him in gratitude for what he did for us.

# Ndai Wona Hama Yakanaka

*(I Have a Good Friend)*

1. Ndai wo-na ha-ma ya-ka-na-ka, ndai wo-na
   *I have a good friend, one who loves me, I have a*
2. Neu-pe-nyu hwa-ngu ndo-hu-to-ra ndo-hu-
   *I give my life, now, all to Je-sus, I sur-*

ha-ma i ne-ru-do. Ndai wo-na
*good friend who loves you too. I have a*
i-sa pa-na Je-su. Neu-pe-nyu
*ren-der my life to him; I give my*

ha-ma ya-ka-na-ka, ndai wo-na
*good friend, one who loves me, I have a*
hwa-ngu ndo-hu-to-ra ndo-hu-
*life, now, all to Je-sus, I sur-*

WORDS: Shona, Zimbabwe; English trans. by Patrick Matsikenyiri
    and Daniel Charles Damon
MUSIC: Shona, Zimbabwe; arr. by Patrick Matsikenyiri

HAMA YAKANAKA
99.99 with Refrain

26

This song talks about finding a friend. In Jesus we find a reliable friend
with whom we can share in confidence.

# Ndi Jesu Chete
### (It's Jesus)

WORDS: Shona, Zimbabwe; English trans. by Patrick Matsikenyiri
and Daniel Charles Damon
MUSIC: Shona, Zimbabwe; arr. by Patrick Matsikenyiri

NDI JESU CHETE
88 with Refrain

di - wa wa - ngu, we mwo-yo wa - ngu, ndi - ye mu -
*one that I love with all of my heart; he is the*

di - wa wa - ngu, we mwo - yo wa - ngu.
*one that I love with all of my heart.*

This song affirms and confidently assures us that it is only Jesus who can give us the good that we have already experienced in life. Be forewarned, no one else can be as committed to us as Jesus is.

# Rujeko
### *(The Light of God Comes)*

*Sing the Refrain once before the leader enters at* **A**.

WORDS: Patrick Matsikenyiri; English trans. by Patrick Matsikenyiri
and Daniel Charles Damon
MUSIC: Patrick Matsikenyiri

RUJEKO
Irr.

*All stanzas enter the chorus in the same manner as shown in stanza 1.*

2. Zva-nya  ko - nja. _____   3. Va - ri  mu-nha - mo. _____
   *In  these  tough    times. ____*      *And  to those  in   trou -ble. _____*

4. I - zwi - ra  Mwa - ri. _____   5. Ku - dzi-nga  di - ma. _____
   *Com-ing  with  God's   word. ___*      *Light-ing  up  the  dark-ness. ___*

6. Je - su  ru-je - ko. _____   7. Ru-je - ko  rwe - i - di. _____
   *Je -sus  is  the    light. _____*      *Je -sus  is  the    life. _____*

8. Ku-ndu-dzi dze - pa - si. _____   9. Ku - ti  ti-nhi - dza. _____
   *To        ev - ery  na - tion. ___*      *Com-ing  to  af - firm us. _____*

10. Ku - va   va - na  va-Mwa-ri. ____  11. Va - ne  ru - po - ne - so. ___
    *To God's child-ren  Je - sus  comes._*   *Com-ing  with sal - va - tion. __*

The light of God comes to the holy ones bringing the message of new life.
In these tough times, to those in trouble, the light comes. Jesus is the light, coming
with salvation to every nation. The bass needs to enhance the choir by solidly
backing it with heavy sound. This song was composed at a workshop during the
liberation struggle in Zimbabwe. The day it was written curfew was imposed
on the Eastern Highlands areas. We were at pains to think how we were going
to get home under those security restrictions. But the light of this song beamed
our way through. We used this song in a documentary film for Sweden.

# Vanomirira Jehova
## (Those Who Wait upon the Lord)

Va - no - mi-ri-ra Je-ho-va, va-no-
*Those who wait up-on the Lord will re-*

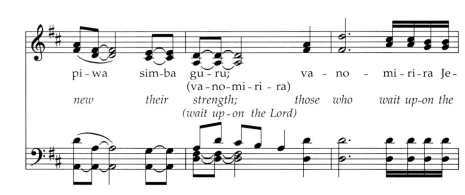

pi-wa sim-ba gu-ru; va - no - mi-ri-ra Je-
(va - no-mi-ri - ra)
*new their strength; those who wait up-on the*
*(wait up-on the Lord)*

ho-va, va-no-pi-wa sim-ba gu-ru. Va-no-
(a - vo - ndi-vo)
*Lord will re - new their strength; they will*
*(they will run)*

WORDS: Trad. Shona, Zimbabwe; English trans. by Patrick Matsikenyiri
and Daniel Charles Damon (Isa. 40:31)
MUSIC: Trad. Shona, Zimbabwe; arr. by Patrick Matsikenyiri

VANOMIRIRA
88.88 11 8.11 8

Trans. and arr. © 2006 Abingdon Press, admin. by The Copyright Co.

This powerful song, taken from Isaiah 40:31, helps us to sustain our faith.
The song gives hope to believers: whatever happens, the Lord will give us
strength if we persist in our endeavor toward perfection. Generally, the motions
imitate what the text is saying. It is common to see Africans joining together
in the motions when they sing songs of this nature. A steady two-beat pulse
makes a good moving beat.

# Wonai
## (Behold)

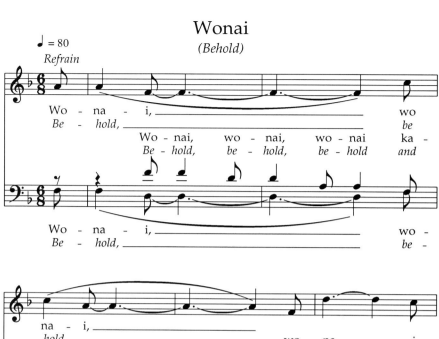

WORDS: Patrick Matsikenyiri; English trans. by Patrick Matsikenyiri
and Daniel Charles Damon (1 Cor. 12)
MUSIC: Patrick Matsikenyiri

WONAI
Irr. with Refrain

Trans. and arr. © 2006 Abingdon Press, admin. by The Copyright Co.

34

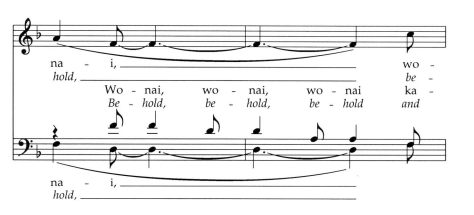

na - i, _____ wo -
*hold,* be -
Wo - nai, wo - nai, wo - nai ka -
*Be - hold, be - hold, be - hold and*

na - i, _____
*hold,* _____

na - i, _____
*hold,* _____ wo - na - i -
ni; wo - nai, wo - nai, wo - nai, *be - hold,* be -
*see; be - hold, be - hold, be - hold,*

na - i, _____
*hold,* _____

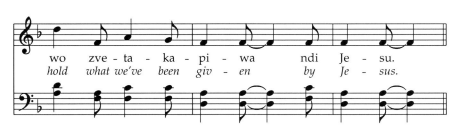

wo zve - ta - ka - pi - wa ndi Je - su.
*hold what we've been giv - en by Je - sus.*

1. Mi - ro - mo ku - dyi - sa ne - ku - shu - ma - i - ra
*Our mouths are for preach - ing and eat - ing with God's*

2. Che - nje - ro ye - pfu - ngwa ku - ndu - dzi dze - se
*We're giv - en our wis - dom for mak - ing good de -*

3. Bva nga - ti - pe - mbe - re - re pa - mbe - ri pa - ke
*Re - joice and be thank - ful be - fore the Lord, our*

va - nhu. Wo - na - i - wo zve - ta - ka - pi - wa ndi
*peo - ple. Be - hold, be - hold what we've been giv - en by*

dze - se. Wo - na - i - wo zve - ta - ka - pi - wa ndi
*ci - sions. Be - hold, be - hold what we've been giv - en by*

Mam - bo. Wo - na - i - wo zve - ta - ka - pi - wa ndi
*Mak - er. Be - hold, be - hold what we've been giv - en by*

Je - su. Ma - o - ka ma - ku - mbo ku -
*Je - sus. Our hands and our feet help us*

Je - su. Chi - mi - ro che - u - nhu che -
*Je - sus. Good lead - ers can help us to*

Je - su. Te - nda - i i - mwi mo - se; mu -
*Je - sus. In cit - y, in vil - lage, with*

fa - mbi - re    va - nge - ri.    Wo - na —    i - wo    zve - ta - ka -
*move  to share  the  gos - pel.    Be - hold,    be - hold  what we've been*

si - na    ru - sa    ru - ro.    Wo - na —    i - wo    zve - ta - ka -
*end    se - gre - ga - tion.    Be - hold,    be - hold  what we've been*

mwo - yo  ye - nyu  va - nhu.    Wo - na —    i - wo    zve - ta - ka -
*sing - ing  and  with  danc - ing.    Be - hold,    be - hold  what we've been*

pi - wa    ndi    Je - su.    Bva    nze - ve    ma -
*giv - en    by    Je - sus.    Our    ears    and    our*

pi - wa    ndi    Je - su.    Chi - di - so  che - vha -
*giv - en    by    Je - sus.    We're  giv - en    com -*

pi - wa    ndi    Je - su.    Mhu - ru - ru  nga - i -
*giv - en    by    Je - sus.    All    voic - es,    all*

dzi - so    ku - tu - nga - mi - re  va - mwe.    Wo - na —    i -
*eyes  guide  us  as  we help each oth - er.    Be - hold,    be -*

nge - ri    chi - si - na  ne - po - ka - no.    Wo - na —    i -
*pas - sion  and  love  for all God's chil - dren.    Be - hold,    be -*

ri - re    pa - mbe - ri  pa  ke  Ma - mbo.    Wo - na —    i -
*peo - ple,  sing prais - es  to  our Mak - er.    Be - hold,    be -*

In 1 Corinthians 12 we see the gifts that have been accorded us by God. Let us be merry and glad, for it could be worse. The song affirms the fact that unity is strength. All people need to work together, not considering one better than the other. "United we stand, divided we fall," becomes a reality in our lives. The bass carries the song. The prolonged bass notes need to be emphasized to give full support to the upper parts.

# Zviro Zvacho Zvanyanya

## (Life Is Broken at Its Core)

WORDS: Patrick Matsikenyiri; English trans. by Patrick Matsikenyiri
and Daniel Charles Damon
MUSIC: Patrick Matsikenyiri; transcribed by Eileen Guenther

ZVIRO ZVACHO
Irr.

Trans. and arr. © 2006 Abingdon Press, admin. by The Copyright Co.

40

Ku-nye-pa kwa-cho,     i - di he - re,
ku-sho - o - ra - na,     i - di he - re,

to.     Zvi-ro zva-cho zva-nya-nya;

Ha - ha,

1   Ku-nyo-mba-na ku,     2    D.S.

Zvo-de mu - na - ma - to.

u - ya - i - mwe-ya,

|     | *literal English (not to be sung)* |
|-----|--------------------------------------|
| 1. Kutadza kani, | sinfulness |
| Kunyepa kwacho, | unfaithfulness |
| Kunyombana ku, | demeaning each other |
| Kushoorana, | lack of appreciation for each other |
| 2. Kuparadzana, | division among each other |
| Ngemadzinza edu, | by tribal line |
| Ngerukanda rwedu, | by our color |
| Ngekuwana kwedu, | by haves and have nots |
| 3. Corruption zvayo, | what of corruption |
| Nzara ne hosha, | hunger and disese |
| Urombo Zvahwo, | even poverty |
| Musiwa zvawo, | even lack of clothes |
| 4. Dollar ro donha, | even the dollar is falling |
| Mitengo yokwira, | prices skyrocketing |
| Dollar ro donha, | even the dollar is falling |
| Mitengo yokwira, | prices skyrocketing |

Anyone who has experienced tough life will relate to the message in this song. When the choir comes to the verses the soloist should be allowed to soar above the choir. Bang it when you come to the refrain, for that affirms the climax of the song. When this song was aired on Zimbabwe radio, many people asked for the text and music. The song received quite a bit of air time on the national radio. Use hand motions invoking the Lord (Uyai Mweya). This song brings the daily lives of the common people into focus. It speaks to people where they are.

# Metrical Index

**LMD (88.87D)**
MWEYA MUYSVENE (22)

**66.66D**
ARIKO NARINI (8)

**77.72D with Hallelujahs**
BANINGYETI (10)

**77.75 with Refrain**
PANO (19)

**88 with Refrain**
NDI JESU CHETE (28)

**88.86.86**
NJALO (4)

**88.88 11 8.11 8**
VANOMIRIRA (32)

**99.99 with Refrain**
HAMA YAKANAKA (26)

**Irregular**
ACHIWONEKA (7)
BABA TINO TENDA (6)
HAKUNA WAKAITA (12)
RUDO (14)
RUJEKO (30)
ZVIRO ZVACHO (39)

**Irregular with Refrain**
NAMATAI (24)
WONAI (34)

# Topical Index

# Scripture Index

**Genesis**
3:1-24                     Zviro Zvacho Zvanyana

**Job**
11:7                       Hakuna Wakaita sa Jesu

**Isaiah**
40:31                      Vanomirira Jehova

**Psalms**
23                         Namatai
133                        Zviro Zvacho Zvanyana
150                        Baningyeti Bayawe

**Matthew**
5:14                       Rujeko
28:20                      Ariko Narini

**Luke**
10:29-37                   Ndai Wona Hama Yakanaka

**John**
3:16                       Ndi Jesu Chete
4:1-42                     Ndai Wona Hama Yakanaka
14:1                       Pano Handiwo Musha
20:1-18                    Mambo Jesu Achiwoneka

**Acts**
2:1-13                     Mweya Mutsvene Uyai Pano
27:35                      Baba Tino Tenda

**1 Corinthians**
12:1-11                    Wonai
13:1-13                    Rudo

**1 Thessalonians**
5:17                       Njalo

# Pronunciation and Performance Guide

The songs in this collection are presented by Patrick Matsikenyiri in Shona, his first language. Patrick speaks Ndebeli and English as well. We worked together on the English translations to make them sound natural. The vowels in Shona sound as follows:

       a = ah     e = eh     i = ee     o = oh     u = oo

You may recognize these as Latin vowels from your voice lessons. This makes Shona a good language for singing. The consonants in Shona are all sounded. There are no silent letters. They sound as in English. The only tricky part of the language for me is the sounding of two consonants together, as in the word "nja - lo." In all words like this, practice pronouncing the consonants together. English has some consonant blends, like "ch," but Shona has a few more.

These songs should generally be performed in parts, accompanied by hand drum and shaker ("hosho" is the Shona word for shaker). Keyboard may be used for support when needed.

Remember to let your body move with this rhythmic music!

# About the Translations

There are three kinds of translations: literal, dynamic equivalence, and paraphrase. The literal translation seeks to give you the exact meaning of the words in the original language. The King James Bible claimed this approach. The New Revised Standard Version follows in that style also. The New International Version tries for the basic meaning of the passage, but is more free with the wording. That style is called "dynamic equivalence." The Living Bible by Ken Taylor is a paraphrase. It goes the farthest from the original language and gains some colloquial ease in the process.

It takes two people to translate a song lyric. One person needs to know both languages, and one should be a poet in the new language. Often our global hymns suffer because no English language poet is engaged to create the final form of the new lyric. For this book, Patrick has given me the exact meaning of the original Shona. I have taken the literal English and put it into what I hope is a natural, singable form. In my process I have tried to stay along the lines of the dynamic equivalence translators, but I occasionally bend in the direction of naturalness in the new language. I focus more on maintaining the orignial meaning and imagery, and less on rhyming. Something is always lost, of course, but when the work is done with care, something can also be gained.

I hope you will enjoy singing these African songs—both in their orignial language and in these new translations.

Dan Damo
July 200

## Dedication and Acknowledgments

I dedicate this work to my family: my parents, the late Diana and Amon Matsikenyiri; to my wife Aves for her unwavering support throughout the project; and to my children, the late Milton and his living siblings Gracious, Farai, Gladys, and Gloria, for their unending support.

I acknowledge Dan Damon's patience in working with me on transcriptions throughout the manuscript while glued to his computer and piano. I am grateful to Eileen Guenther for her initial suggestion that I publish my works, and for her transcriptions of two songs in this collection.

I acknowledge the bishops and the Annual Conference in Zimbabwe, and St. Peter's United Methodist Church Choir, Mutare, for its contribution to the recording.

I acknowledge Patty Jones, Nathan Kennedy-Gibbons, and Lindsay Ireland for helping to coordinate my visits to churches in the Pacific Northwest Annual Conference, and the late Marvel Walter, who coordinated my tour of California-Nevada Annual Conference churches.

A big "thank you" goes to the president and staff of Shenandoah University, who pioneered my visits to churches and institutions, and to Wesley Theological Seminary, Drew University, Adrian College, and Africa University for their participation as a testing ground for the music prior to publication.

To the many who played a role and have not been mentioned, I say "thank you" very much.

Patrick Matsikenyiri, F.A.B.I.

# St. Peter's United Methodist Choir, Mutare, Zimbabwe

## Patrick Matsikenyiri, Music Director and Leader's Voice

### Sopranos

1. Anasu Mhondoro
2. Tendai Magadaire
3. Nyasha Sanyahumbi
4. Tsitsi Mutangi
5. Tsitsi Makande
6. Selisa Mapungwana
7. Sandra Mutowo
8. Segelyn Maranga
9. Bertha Mashingaldze
10. Tapiwa Munyebvu
11. Gloria Mutee
12. Beauty Marangwanda
13. Tambubzai Sauramba
14. Shiella Munguma
15. Josephine Gimane
16. Esther Munyebvu
17. Rufaro Tumbare

### Altos

1. Rufaro Matimati
2. Tatenda Matimati
3. Victoria Murimba
4. Georgina Mupunga
5. Tambudzai Jarvawani
6. Grace Taziana
7. Abigail Mundondo
8. Susan Mareya
9. Emily Marage
10. Angeline Haparari
11. Nyasha Matasva
12. Margaret Machiri
13. Catherine Chimboza
14. Beauty Chimhutu
15. Phillippa Miaka

### Tenors

1. Trevor Munyebvu
2. Gift Mukono
3. Godwin Zitsanza
4. Blessing Bello
5. John Munyebvu
6. Taona Mutengo
7. Tendai Tumbare
8. Shadreck Mrangwanda
9. Moses Marange

### Basses

1. David Chieza
2. Lovemore Mareya
3. Ephraim Magadaire
4. Owen Matanhire
5. Tauringana Simango
6. Brighton Mhandu
7. Mack Nhema
8. Patrick Matsitkenyiri

### Instrumentalists

Drum: Trevor Munyebvu
Hosho: Ephraim Magadaire